The Principle of Rapid Peering

Also by Sylvia Legris

THE PRINCIPLE
of
RAPID PEERING

Sylvia Legris

with illustrations by the author

A New Directions Paperbook Original

Manufactured in the United States of America
First published as a New Directions Paperbook (NDP1594) in 2024

Library of Congress Cataloging-in-Publication Data
Names: Legris, Sylvia, author, illustrator.
Title: The principle of rapid peering / Sylvia Legris;
with illustrations by the author.
Other titles: Principle of rapid peering (Compilation)
Description: New York, NY: New Directions Publishing Corporation, 2024.
Identifiers: LCCN 2023043038 | ISBN 9780811237642 (paperback)`
Subjects: LCGFT: Poetry.
Classification: LCC PR9199.3.L3945 P75 2024 |
DDC 811/.54—dc23/eng/20230922
LC record available at https://lccn.loc.gov/2023043038

10 9 8 7 6 5 4 3 2 1

New Directions Books are published for James Laughlin
by New Directions Publishing Corporation
80 Eighth Avenue, New York, NY 10011

ndbooks.com

for Guy

So we really are lost, in a very odd way. We need to find our way through the landscape in order to draw the map, and at the same time we need to draw the map in order to find our way through the landscape.

— Inger Christensen
from *The Condition of Secrecy*
(tr. Susanna Nied)

Contents

Occasionally the Field of Possibilities

PART II

PART I

The Air Is Seeded

Voucher Specimen [1]

Field-pinned in the month of purification.
The month of salt-cure and heart attack.
The year of rats and shivering pinions.

Candlemas heralds thunderstorm asthma.
Woodchucks and infectious shadows.
A spring of glycerol suspension.

Aspen trembles flames and owlet moths,
yellow underwings and flames to dispel
hearsay and off-season night flying.

Viscum Album

1

Plants and potent juice.
Mist and droppings.

Birdlime.
Missel thrush.

Beak.
Or of the nose.

Sap.
Or of the skin.

Blear.
Vapor.

The air is seeded.
Contagion or prayer.

2

Ring a ring o' roses.
Broom root and mistletoe.
Ligneous chatterers.
Lungs halo March.

3

Skint wit; scantier spring.
Housed in bindweed.
With-wind-invasive.
Aggressive triple-glaze.

4

April enters blank-leaved.
Snowbanked, eco-dormant.

Waxwings initiate budburst.
Mountain ash and winterberry.

Balsam poplar a study in starling leaf-out.
Western larch lurches grey jay and blue.

April Fools is blowing snow.
Good Friday cloudy with flock calls.

5

Stigmatized by the confusion-chorus.
Wistful New World sparrows.

The shelterbelt a stormcocked cock-up.
A three-noted cluster song.
A varied trill transmission.

6

April 21st and winter gravels into spring.
A season of *restless, puny, energy.*
Frantic kinglets, freeloading plants.
Nest-squatters in their element.

7

What the wind carries is up for grabs:
plastic, elastic, particulate-filtering paper.

14th Street a molt of latex and medical-grade nitrile.
Walkers cautious-walk the two-meter wingspan walkway.

Runners flappable as flycatchers.
Ill at ease eavesdroppers.
Spittle in the slipstream.

8

The spurious specious present.
The calendar sloshes toward May.
Late April grueling snow and deciduous indecision.
Leaf mold, wilt mush, the days all fall down.

9

A calendrical clot.
A six-week intercalation.
A thousand-hour schism.
An embolism.

10

May is self-digesting sky,
intrusive granite with floaters.

Necrotic flowerbeds,
cartilage-grinding wind,
an unremitting erroneous huff.

11

... the sinking vessel of the landscape.

Blast-bagged and walking windward.
Peripheral foliage, last year's cavity nests,
witches' broom avoided like ...

12

A segue:
Seed-dispersal
by upward-inflected whip-bur.

The trouble-excreting thrush,
the implicated junco,
the hectoring
venison-hawk vector.

Pickthankless days
parasitize days.

Ground Truth

A Spray of Foliage; Rapidly Beating Wings

Ground truth reveals scattered cloudy wing,
scattered clouded sulphur,
mourning cloaks of water-droplet clouds.

Without Noticing It until the Moment It Moved

Junes of storm basins and retention ponds.
Bewildering wild deceits.
Julys of sludge and flaccid rain.
Albumeny sloughs.

                    *

A blackbird wakes and with it the urge to forage.
Hatched with a typographic knack.
An egg of brown and black hieroglyphs.

                    *

One season masks the season to come.
Clouds gestating storms.
A pupa gestures moths past and moths forthcoming.
A larval, tutelary sky.

                    *

A gust front of rising and falling inflection.
A stammering draft of dorsal vessel action.
A flight of wing-shaped alary muscles.
Gathering hemolymph.
An open circulatory downpour.

These Birds and All Kindred Species
That Roost in the Reeds

Low-nesting below goldenrod.
The jaundiced ones.
The brood-parasitized.
The brood parasites.

*

The nest-absconders.
The misapprehended—
for wormseed mustard,
for late yellow locoweed.

*

The ones who engender yellow
umbrage
among drab Old Worlders.

*

The wren-antagonists,
yellow beneath the meniscus
(twayblade, tickseed, bog orchid).

*

The big voice flashers.
Wings of metal and night.

Take the Case of the Meadowlark

Peak gust and west of July.
Wind is full-song singing wings,
full-on whistling grass saturation.

The aftercast (neither wet-bulb nor
oldfield lark, not dry punch, not
diablo wind) an atlas of starling-

like neglect, flock-overlook.

*

Emily Dickinson wrote:
"Split the Lark—and you'll find the Music—"

*

Sturnella neglecta

> *... the sweet singer of the plains ...*

An air parcel of western meadowlark.
A sky of spreading yellow.

Gape-jawed, famished,
May lifts and drags dregs
of April, Aurora Borealis, Corona Borealis ...

Accelerating notes,
a melodious jumble.
On the wing
        ... *singing,*
          as if under pressure ...

A Melodic Expectation

A day transpires in an hour.
Purple prairie clover,
nodding beggarticks,
alighting cabbage whites.

*

Before slough transmutation
there was knobbed and kettled,
trifolium-forage and bloat-stop,
a pretense of yellow clover and nature.

Common Summer Resident of the Deeper Sloughs; Frequenting the Willow-Edged Sloughs

Nests strung among vertical shoots.
(In the not unmusical reed beds.)

A brackish depression.
Reedmace and punk.

Wind couplets and sun
behind a weak rotation.

*

Another funnel cloud advisory
dispelled by bruised goldenrod
emanating air of wild carrot

... as if to choke the balance of the sky ...

As if to baffle wetland edge and vanishing point,
an impending heat mirage displaced
by blinking brome and eyelash grass,
plaine watery feakes of foxtail.

Smell Giveaway (Isabelline)

Flats of flat-topped aster host
a row of black dorsal spots,
a faint flame forewing,
Pyrrharctia isabella.

Arcturus and a fizzling instar.
August of loud fumes.
August of scent volatility.
Artemisia's canescent array:

an underside of grey-yellow absinthe,
sagebrush of wing-spanning panicles,
hindwings of wind-pollinated whiffs.
An aromatic mimicry-ring.

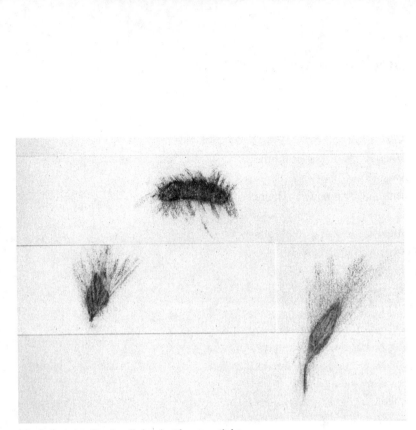

P. Isabella caterpillar (woolly bear) with grass spikelets

Grass Veneer [1]

Sensu lato:
When moth surpasses moth.
Awn-tips and awn-points.
Lemma with a crown of hairs.

Midvein to a fringe of fibrous roots.
A costal margin of sheep fescue.

*

Ad libitum:
The saltgrassed subapical.
The wide-streaked alkali cordgrass.
The aster-feeding immaculate hairgrass.

Hollow bluegrass culms, a plying wind.
Webworms glume the inflorescence meristem.

Free-floating woolly bears

Grass Veneer [2]

Wind slivers silver and longitudinal.

A storm-edge of discal stripe
cut off at the subterminal line.

Forewing with a triangular apex.
A smoke-white hindwing.
Five dark spots loom.

*

An oblique view through a ventral window.
Fescue of six weeks.

C. praefectellus is false melic chaffing moth.
Distal floret with scale-tooth.
A scabrous-awned derangement.

Mottled grass and dotted angled lines.
Moth more monocotyledonous than moth.

As If These Objects Were Moving
and the Bird Itself Were Quiet

Wind spins strobili,
spherical seed cones,
bird cherries and wind-
indicating birds.

Chewing's fescue and creeping red,
tussocks of dipsy-doodling blackbirds.

*

A forward-jerking flock fulcrum.
Lawns of any and armyworms.
Cutworms, codling moths.
Gulletfulls of larvae.

Sun guzzles quick down August's throat.
Final flagging gags of heat.

Smell Giveaway (Threes on long stalks)

Galium triflorum.
Gallium sphinx caterpillar.

The breathing swale trails
the horned and hovering,

the sweet-scented bedstraw,
the ascending bedstraw hawkmoth.

Dusk-feeding nightfall,
a bullbatting nighthawk,

a loggerhead of grebe and shrike,
pipit pipit pipit.

Voucher Specimen [2]

Ground truth reveals wing-brittle wind.
Limbs flailing in sixes of constriction.

Nothing is as was predicted.
Obedience proportional
to proximity of the pin.

Relax! (*Shh* ... relax.)
Swale-swollen the lungs
are two-brooded,
two altruistic balloons.

Two pops and the air will clear.
Another season on a polyvoltine calendar,
spring and spring and spring and spring.

Forecast Issued 5:00 AM CST
Sunday 27 December 2020

1

1:00 PM.

Slimmon Slough and the sky
is a slate lake, a swimming bitmap,

trout-perch and sturgeon,
gravity grey,

a downward acceleration,
a cowl of brushed-chrome

pigeon, cool grey
in 30% saturation.

2

Pine-pollen snow.
Hawk pellets of spew and feather.
Midmorning groundcast shows bitter dock,
basin of bifurcated roots,
unbranched ice needles.

3

At 0500 hours
a Mercury-void

sediments
the meander.

The undercast
reads underground

a prima vista,
epifauna phonics

on pause,
tallgrass in repose.

Forecast Issued 6:00 AM CST
Friday 1 January 2021

7:00 AM the sky a hypothetical blue,
blue outside the geographic range of blue,
accidental, a blue-grey gnatcatcher.

Sunrise at 9:15.
Wind chill as much anecdote as geometry.
Breath of photonic ice crystals,
iridescence at minus twenty-two.

Turquoise, prismatic, hoarfrost
flashes foraging magpies,
one for sorrow, two for mirth,
gusts northeast in reverse,
feathers riming windward.

Occasionally the Field of Possibilities

An Anatomy in Four Seasons

The First Spring of Covid

Kinglets overshoot the calendar,
the first seeds dispersing
of the many-seasoned malaise.

Extraordinary but for the ordinary
uncertain medley of location notes.

Wind out of G-sharp.
Waxwings parleying with stern nature.
A blizzard that fails to drown the shrill air.

Below Optimist Hill a sandbar like an artic barge.
The river's pulmonary pull, slump-banked with short-
winded breeze, an epidermis of pancake ice.

Breath of ground-glass opacity.
Deflective impressions of storm.
An aeonian April of splintered sun arc.

The First Summer

Spring's undying debate suspended in interpleural space.

The sky doubles down with a butchery of rain,
seedlings slaughtered amid monotonous water.

Every sodden second another watershed moment
exits the lung-stream, antediluvian elms desperate for breath.

Solstice, the air stands still, the branchlets grasp.
Summer under a canopy of arterial despair.

The First Fall

First the damping down of the high bush sympathetic strings.
Then the autonomic nervous system's harmonic flight.
A spinney of deciduous windpipes enters acoustic abscission.
Leaves fall silent, the air takes an enigmatic breather
among low bush cranberry, dwarf bog cranberry,
and the pale pinesap pitch of wobbly homeostasis.
... Meanwhile the river
lackadaisically rights itself to the shifting tempo of sandbar.

The First Winter

The already heard tapping of the bronchial tree.
The *déjà entendu* of the deoxygenated orchestral.
A winter that registers the distance from airborne to archive.
Vitrines of snow globes with bone chip snow.
Winter with an elliptical flight path.
The perturbing reverb of birds striking glass.

A Rolling Moth Etymology

1. Flight and only flight is a delicately orchestrated
   irrational response to a moth.

2. To unpack a fear of moths (mottephobia)
   is to open a pandora's voice box of rumor and legend.
   While performing an aria from Handel's *Messiah*,
   a moth flew into a soprano's mouth.
   "I know that my Redeemer liveth," she sangeth, and fished the moth out.

3. All breath stops for moths.
   To live within moth-spinning windows is to live under pupal arrest.
   To become unfettered from the tyranny of flutter
   necessitates deft intervention of pickle jar and pluck.

4. Moth-eaten from the 14c.
   A nocturnal devouring.
   A hankering for knits on hangers.

5. Nits, gnats, an etymon of moth is midge.
   A collision of no-see-um and no escapin'.

6. Also see maggot,
   the absurdity of flesh,
   the fragile feelers.

7. The reciprocal duties of hospitality are not lost on a moth.
   Take the populous poplar, a popular host—
   the spotted tussock moth caterpillar feasts all season
   and where there were leaves leaves lace, a brocade of moonlight.

8. Fall is to summer as pupa is to larva.
   Dormancy is the season between winter and willow.

9   Ditto the calendar of moths.
    Buck moth after Juno.
    Half-wing and full Luna.

10 Moth wings write the fingers with graphite.
    Unearthly grease DNAs the moth's release into night.
    Fool's gold dust-shimmer.
    The rust of decaying fabric.

11 The original title of Virginia Woolf's *The Waves* was *The Moths*.
    While moth-hunting is best done under a full moon,
    the illumination required to write a book of great worth
    is inversely proportional to that required to trap a moth.

Lesser grapevine looper liftoff

Occasionally the Field of Possibilities [1]

Is branch-spined,
a folded-leaf feeder,
a spatial array
of buckeye larvae,
snapdragons pulling
a pollinator-cue,
orange prolegs
telegraphing mirror-
image eyespots,
a macula lutea sun.

Occasionally the Field of Possibilities [2]

Is disruptive coloration,
yellow concentric rings
around a single eye,
a fovea centralis
of seed cones & pollen cones,
closely packed juniper seeds,
a Polyphemus moth with
urticating bristles & needles
with fine stomata lines, a nexus
of cone axis & host pine.

Occasionally the Field of Possibilities [3]

Is a field of 30,000 ommatidia,
a composite eye
eyeing woodruff & pale persicaria,
ten conspicuous eyespots
bisecting summer & pupation,
the line severing dusk & night,
the night flying hawkmoths,
is tapetal-mirrored,
a reflective tracheal network,
a superpositional glow.

Occasionally the Field of Possibilities [4]

Is a coevolved canopy
of wing scale & leaf,
a broadband acoustic cloak
deflecting echo & foe,
wavelengths of powder & light,
a cloud of stacked platelets,
a thin-film percussion,
hair-penciled & interlinear,
sparkling archaic sun moths,
a microlepidopterous register.

Occasionally the Field of Possibilities [5]

Is night-active & pupillary,
wing-fringe grazing cornea,
small moth repetitions
in an orbit of sequestration notes,
thick scale vestiture,
glassy, bluegrass-hosted,
rain-impermeable with snow-
veined forewings, a loop
of sequestration notes,
a small moth repetition.

Occasionally the Field of Possibilities [6]

Is a current of candles & dawn
half a clockface ago,
a Yablochkovian glow
of carbon-arcing waxwings,
match twigs, linstock boughs,
a sky of combustible fruit
tinders a river of ruined craters,
winter on its last legs,
a winter of monthlessness,
winter with plants in the belly.

Occasionally the Field of Possibilities [7]

Is a complicity
of ruckus & pinion,
is the pollen grain music
of a microstructure of modified hairs,
light-interfering wings,
sight-singing by structural coloration,
a scalic descent
down a microscopic edifice
of struts & holes, wings close
& the moth composes.

An Anatomy in Four Seasons

The Second Spring of Covid

Rapid melt waters the crosstalk between sleep and wake.
Dreams of rising water fuse with flicker and flare.
The brain turns the off switch to switchgrass,
long drought dry-drowns short drought,
the sleeping mind wakes to the membrane crack
of cloud-to-lung lightning, hammering imaginings
—woodpecker architecture, an incursion of starlings,
skull in thrall to secondary cavity nesters.

The Second Summer

The post-winter grousing of melt and pout
(a spring of noncommittal petulance)
overpowered by bitterroot's parched optimism.

Fleece-flowering headwinds,
drought-lungs of goutweed,
a hydrologic imbalance of geraniums.

A full flower moon ignites a conflagration
of flight-feeding nightjars,
prevailing winds of asthma and ash,
ophthalmic throb of far-off conifer smoke.

The Second Fall

The summer of brimstone and smoking trees capitulates
to the heavy-limbed galumph of glucose-depletion.
A weave of starving leaves leaves not a breath
of the respiratory-distressed topsoil exposed.
Prayers blow by like the guarantee of rain that never came.
Prayers like low-layered clouds, a high-haze horizon
of upstroke and downstroke, an unnerving of wings.
Meanwhile the river follows the folly
of what the eye can't see can't hurt.

The Second Winter

Denuded timorous aspen.
Last winter's terminal buds.
Bud scale scars.

A morbid absorption of pith solid and bark,
poplars stressed with conspicuous lenticels,
the river's thready pulse,
the perpetual porous passage
of perilous air into imperilled membrane.

Occasionally the Field of Possibilities [8]

Is a rebirding of the bilateral lung field,
is pulmonary gas exchange as slough wind,
tissue-permeable, a parallel shiver,
a perpendicular burst of cattails.

Occasionally the field of possibilities
is the erstwhile bronchial understory
in an iteration of brash Icteridae,
grasslocked & syllabilizing,
a twelve-bird octave, a slew
of ground-foraging blackbirds.

PART II

"Walk," was my answer, "I definitely must, to invigorate myself and to maintain contact with the living world ..."

> — Robert Walser, from *The Walk*
> (tr. Christopher Middleton with
> Susan Bernofsky)

The Walk, or The Principle of Rapid Peering
(Also known as A Trek of Air, A Living Poem)

1. Like birds that perch and wait passively

An almanac of slow erosion,
the daily repetitive browse.

Weather inertia,
a protracted diapause,
the river beats a shallow rise and fall.

Earworms of looper moths and scripted arches,
a modulation more barometer than memory.

Frost forces flock cohesion,
the riverbank a diminuendo of willow,
the sky an aerosol of indifference.

*

Shy birds dawdle an abandonment
of abundant winter residents.
The same frozen stance since the first weeks
of borrowed days and dark-feathered sky.

Those kinds of birds that roost and wait passively.
A studied shift from one steadfast pose to another.
An intent eye on the ground.

... a low lurking percher ...
... a *quit-quit-quit* from a thicket ...
... a reedy song but no sighting ...

Hermitic
as a thrush,
the first, short warble of spring is nearly thus ...

Out of earshot tulip shoots
pursue the eternal
vernal rosiness.

A forecast of meagre sun exalting noble gas,
true air space with a half-inch leeway.
A forecast of insulated glazing, PVC,
little noise to mitigate.

Spring through fixed windows,
spring of ill stars and false-
starting Solomon's seal,

a panorama of perennials
poised to toss the towel in,
a convolution of roots and wind.

Gone the intercostal-straining winds,
the minus-fifty winter theatrics.
Seasonal wind-exchange
yields windows of viscid rain.
The horizontal movement of water
a conjunction of slurry and wind.

Balsam, white spruce ... Anemophilous pine trees
translate secondary winds into local winds,
a spring of pollination by hard-pressed respiration,
ever the dispersal of evergreen-nesting sparrows.

                    *

Sedum after sedum re-emerges unhindered.
Unchecked the stonecrops: the gold moss,
the variegated, the glaucous greens and succulent.

Unchecked the salvia, the Siberian bugloss,
the crawling ground of cutworm larvae.
Unchecked more of the same habitually habituated rabbits.

Unchecked the sun illumines a sharp wick call,
a chattering flight song,

a bitone with a question mark,
will-ya? will-ya?

... repair to the great marshes ...
... prepare for incessant motion ...

"... simplicity most ancient to walk on foot ..."

The field of our work is the region immediately about us.

Boulevards and parks,
trails on both sides of the South Saskatchewan,
naturalized sites, conservation sites ...

*

The feet trudge the path of the eyes.

Vouch for scarcely frozen trails skirted by galvanic tamaracks,
the previous fall's needles a carpet of #2 pins.

Vouch for garrulous waxwings captivating powerlines,
mesmerizing middle C and rising,
coloratura clouds.

Vouch for the rich acoustic world of moths
fallen silent, streets of pupal stillness,
bodies suspended in glycerol sleep.

Vouch for the condition of air.
Old air? Bad air? Malarial?
Air of endless revision
and infinite transmission,
News World Air, CBC and CNN Air,
Regional Broadcast Air.

Cloying air like the air in a funeral home,
or an unfinished basement, or a root cellar.
Air that carries the DNA of many lungs.

      *

How many variations on Nature?

Vouch for:
Wildlife—Flora—Fauna
Landscape—Countryside—Natural surroundings

Vouch for:
Cosmos—Macrocosm—Scenery
Outdoors—Natural history—Forest

Vouch for a city of composite eyes.
How many million ommatidia?
Through the trees blows an extraocular wind.
Eyes with wings.
Wings with eyespots.
The holding pattern prevaricates.

*

So re-emerges the air-swindler,
the sometime airflow-ambivalent.

A coalition of plant fibre
and hollow bone,
a hybrid zone
in a deep-lobed
lethally beautiful register
of Old World stavesacre.

Vouch for 173 species of grass,
herbaceous with the poly-
saccharide clitter of exoskeleton,
each with a corresponding suborder
songbird pitch.

Chitin, cellulose, keratin,
a stridulation
of probing beaks and proboscises,
wings with bones and wings
longways veined,
phalanx-like spikelets,
airborne seeds.

*

Navigate a fogbank of seeds—
a wind tide of Achilles
tendon-deep elm seeds,
double-winged samaras,
hermaphroditic basswood,
a wade of plumy achenes.

Navigate another season
of reasonable doubt.
Weather is disorder,
syndromes of pollination and diffusion,
fruitless overwintering,
a gravity of confusion.

Syndrome:
a running together,
where several paths meet,
where nature converges with words.

<< *Wind* >>

Wind is tympanic,
percussive air,
a wing-scale libretto,
a silver-spotted ghost moth

or a premonition
of a clack and chatter chack call,
a red-winged blackbird's
two-part alarm whistle.

Self-seeding wind
is a wind of ever-replenishing breath.

Speedwell wind, Veronica spine, a wind
of windfalls and bird's-eye hindsight.

Impetuous direct-sowing wind
plies impatient birds with a beak's-reach of seed.

Windward a fledgling bed
of mauve belladonna hybrid.

Leeward low larkspur
out-upslurs the downwind

lark sparrow, the grassland
lark bunting, a contrary

delphinium wind—
butterfly blue, bee blue,

blue-centred
blue dawn.

*

Wind is a metamorphosis
of infinite cycles of breath.

Shelf clouds lined
with an evolution of air,

book lungs and book gills,
a library of respiration

(the passive, the active,
by spiracle by stoma by lung),

the inner floristic,
Holarctic rind.

<<*wind*>>

Unrooted in the substrate.

Day after day barely submersed,
some sort of emergent pondweed,
blunt-leaved lacking lacunae.

Day after day of open bog,
prostrate sedge with edges
gust-scuffed dull.

Feet fall on nubby ground,
seed casings, avian moult,
an excess of exuviae—

the instinctive cyclic shedding.

A loose-leaf ledger of deciduousness.
Pages of caducous sepals and organs

easily detached, the falling cadence
of leaves and departures, dead leaf

scrolls of flakes and scales, months
and months of gratuitous sloughing.

*

Months and months mediated by disruptive patterning.
Familiar landscape sunk into familiar landscape.

Poplar branches with twigs of twig-mimicking caterpillars.
Maple seeds masquerading as day-flying moths.

Elm trees wrangle rings of past and pestilence.
Geometer larvae measure the earth with cautious respiration.

... repair to swale and slough ...
... repair to upland and riverbank ...

2. Birds continually in motion

Vouch for another precipitous liftoff.
Vouch for another misleading season,
another climatic about-face.

A warm front swaps out cold air for singing air.
Trailing edge of a vesper warble.
A provisional perch on a short chant.
A descending riparian wetland scale.
Sagebrush scrub, wolf willow, pussy willow,
choke cherry and green ash.

An optical field of pasqueflower,
spindles of lavender and grey.
Snow legs give way to wet mud legs,
rain mixed with snow,
slush on daubs of grassy sand,
wind whooshing the earth's ears.

Eyes forage the ground.
Rosehips, juniper berries,
coagulated drizzle.

Frost just sufficient
to form a lens of ice on standing water.

<<*Light*>>

Come spring an ocular transition,
longer days enter the pupil,
the cornea acclimatizes

from light under ice to light over water,

the dark retinal back of winter
a floral thaw of leaf and plumage,
rain and a river of rods and cones.

*

Come sun a maintopmost angle.
A crow's eye's wide ambit.
Edge habitat, parkland
on a periphery of marsh,
a gambit of dead sticks and bark,
walls of mud and wintered weeds.

The bird's eye turns as the neck turns.
Trunk torsion,
branches of radial nerve pain.
Trees' bark marked with old grievances,
lightning quarrels, 48-knot winds.

A field of manyfold enhanced vision.
Tetrachromatic—ultraviolet, red, green, blue.
Fourth-cone shortwave sensitivity.

Blackbirds, magpies, meadowlarks, grackles.
A high-contrast backdrop of green.
A dramatic foliage spectrum
in an avifauna-specific script
of iridescence
and UV-reflecting objectives.

<<*light*>>

Variegated grass notes and graceful sedge,
scraped hollows of sprangletop and cordgrass,
bulrush, ditchgrass, water-plantain.

A nearby slough with a solo oriole,
a mixed chorus of blackbirds,
knotted rush and a monocot ostinato:
duckweed waterweed bur-reed
duckweed waterweed bur-reed . . .

Below the slow-flowing troposphere a clovered edge,
an agglomeration of greens and yellows,
hodgepodge of water and sky, mud and blue.

Plants that float and water-striding insects,
ticks, fleas, feather mites, lice—parasites
with *loose membership in the roving aggregation of bird*s . . .

*

A nesting stretch of swamp thistle, coralroot,
yellow bird's-foot trefoil.

Nape feathers of marsh marigold,
a crown of buttercup yellow.

A crest of red samphire—
a stubble of inconspicuous flowers.

Shoulder swatches of scarlet paintbrush
    wave a flash of yellow flax ...

    A yellow-headed wailing trill,
        a flap and glide, a nasal *whaaah* ...

        A red-winged *chek* call over water,
            a breeze of tricolor synchronization ...

    *

Blackbirds and crows with a cortical vocabulary
of a hundred million colors—
opalescent orbital rings,
kaleidoscopic threat displays,
preen glands refracting light on wet feathers.

Blackbirds and crows with museum conscience.
An archive of tightly packed neurons,
immodest order amidst a complex jargon
of x's and k's, water-welling vowels.

An archive of the presence and absence
of creatures and beasts, plunderers and prey,
of the rapid-wing swing of faunal boundaries.

An archive of floral surroundings,
of "... the green and luscious embellishments of trees ..."

<<*Green*>>

Greenbelts, shade trees,
thin-walled nests suspended from forked twigs.

Deep-cupped nests in roadside groves,
grasslands that muddy slants of wild and tame.

Roosts of sumac, of shrubby sandbar willow,
root-lined nests in the underwings of elms.

Lichen, mosses, spruce needles,
aquatic vegetation and waterlogged leaves,
basket nests concealing reveries of green.

Birds with a sensory consciousness of green.

Green in open light,
green at dusk,
an itinerant retention of larvae and grass.

Pellucid aphid green,
winged or wingless.

Cabbage loopers, cabbage whites,
a proliferation of leaf caterpillars
by dint of an eradication of green.

                    *

Tallgrass green is grey-blue bluestem.
Rough hairgrass is flyaway,
more curlew brown than green-winged teal.
Under kidney-shaped clouds Kentucky blue grass green
has the mottled patina of a Crambid snout moth.

Leaves and grass in unstable shades of green:
praying mantis, emerald, mint,
shamrock, algae, jade,
malachite, spring.

The frequency of green is the frequency
of grackles alighting lawn.
Plumage flips lenticular
from purple to blue to the green
sheen of a Brewer's blackbird.

*

Green larvae submit
to the nastic movement of plants,
a stimulus of hover and gaze,
of wingtip annexing air,
a reflex of droop or drop.

Eyes blaze.
Eyes seize and hold fast.

Blackbird point of view
is beak point,
punctum beccus,
where beak
points the eye's target.

<<*green*>>

Nondenominational winds blow east-rising birds west.
Diurnal flyers emulate a streamlined skyline.

Black eyes reflect a bony-socketed sun,
yellow eyes mirror light on trees.

From below *the only moving thing*
is fair weather cumulus,

clear sky with low-loft yellow
eye-rings.

A harmonized sweep
of blackbirds
freely flits
striated banks,
flits the smooth
involuntarily muscled
gesticulations
of pressure gradient
provoking water.

*

Plumage eclipses river,
eclipses sky and light,

tidal volume a sum of air
displaced by flight,

a spirometry curve of abrupt
wing beats and up

and down undulations.

Ground truth insinuates
micrometeorite dust.

A sunrise of black and yellow birds
succeeds a sky of rare noctilucent clouds,
feathers vaporous with electric tension,
a speculation of blue.

                    *

Blackbirds, magpies, meadowlarks, grackles,
a roving aggregation of Icterids

            —peckish, rapid-peering—

stops over
at a park with a panoptical view of slough ...

stops over
at an isolation of drought-tolerant grama grass,
heaving breath of needle and thread grass,
white aspen with harsh weather singes,
a vigilant orbit of woodpecker holes.

The staging ground is set . . .

Mountain ash berries,
hackberries,
linden seed.
Edible grains and grass seed.

Languorous grasshoppers,
malingering beetles,
lethargic snails and all inclinations
of sluggish larvae—
caterpillars, motionless grubs.

*

*Observation shows that commoner birds may be divided into two
categories with regard to their method of obtaining food:*

1. those who wait passively for food to approach them;
2. the almost continually in motion rapid-peering birds (many from the
    family *Icteridae*) whose target of desire is stationary.

*

The rapid-peerer's eyes turn
as the head changes position.

The eyes focus the beak,
the instrument of capture.

The rapid-peerer's eyes mimic
digitigrade locomotion.

The head follows the feet,
quick moves, to, fro.

Feet with an intelligence of texture,
bark, branch, gravel, soil.

        *

The staging ground is set

for an apneic suspension
of wind-disbelief,

birds with eyes
with wings

grounded
by uninterrupted air,

birds on an obstinate
eyeballing walk,

birds with excesses of vigor,
quests for order,

migrating memories
of green and grass.

False Chronologies with Birds and Moths

The idea of calendar is off the table.
The brain reconstructs a lawlessness of seasons,
an outbreak of unreliable chronologies.
The present never more specious than the present,
trees fully leafed one moment and defoliated the next.

The sky evokes wingtip vortices of three years ago,
crow instability displaced by bird-induced drag.
Mid-level convergence of a hundred species of birds,
an implausible cloud of winter-stoics and sun-wooers.

Flight over ravine, corkscrew loop, a narrow-spined valley.
Wind carries a bird through nine calendars a year.
A wind-chorale corrals a society of birds, overlapping flight paths,
a single spring a swoop of twenty thousand abbreviated hours,
seed-dispersal by sustained wind, a sustained anemochory chorus.

The path of the bird's flight mirrors the bird's mind moving.
Zigzagging supraciliary treetops, plotting a river of hyperpixelation.
An oily lens filters foliage and green water magenta, the bird's eye
espies rising-sun curvatures of leaf-curled larvae, espies
the dazzle of light on cuticle, a once-married underwing's
reniform spot, nano-structured, an invisible wing-spectrum.

The dream inward dreams flight before eclosion,
the moth before pupal case, the bird before shell.
The dream inward dreams the poem before the poem.
All the lights in the sky are off when this happens.

"Recollections of the Future"

Weather was measured in calories.

The former metabolism serenaded the ice cube tray that once held ice cubes made from the water of the last known hailstones.

The lemonade had more air than ice and more ice than lemons.

Flavor was rationed and what flavor there was was scraped from under the fingernails into a small vial and left outside the door for collection by a government employee wearing a suit of indeterminate fabric.

All the lights in the sky were off when this happened.

After dark you could choose between eating and not tasting or sleeping and not dreaming.

If you tasted and dreamt at the same time you would sleepwalk and sleep-eat but all you would find in the fridge was a long-squeezed lemon half and a fingernail scraping that was lost then found but unaccounted for.

If you ate and slept at the same time you would wake to sirens and loud knocks and diminishing weather on the other side of the door.

Notes

I've been very conscious that some of these poems written during the height of Covid are re-entering the "bird and lung field" of my poems in *Pneumatic Antiphonal* (New Directions, 2013). "An Anatomy in Four Seasons" (*"The First Winter"*), "Occasionally the Field of Possibilities [8]," and a couple of lines in part one of "The Walk..." make direct reference to lines in that collection.

Several of the poems in the second section are titled directly or as paraphrases after passages in either Joseph Grinnell's essay "The Principle of Rapid Peering, in Birds" or in Ernest E. Thompson's *The Birds of Manitoba*.

"Viscum Album": In number six, "restless, puny energy" is from an observation by ornithologist Elliott Coues about the ruby-crowned kinglet, as cited by Grinnell in "The Principle of Rapid Peering, in Birds." In number eleven, "the sinking vessel of the landscape" is from Miroslav Holub's poem "The end of the world," translated from the Czech by Ewald Osers, in *Poems Before & After*.

"Take the Case of the Meadowlark": "the sweet singer of the plains" and "singing, / as if under pressure" are from Thompson's *The Birds of Manitoba*. Emily Dickinson's line "Split the Lark—and you'll find the Music—" is from her poem 861.

"Common Summer Resident of the Deeper Sloughs...": "as if to choke the balance of the sky" is from Holub's poem "Landscapes," translated by Ewald Osers, in *Poems Before & After*. The line "plaine watery feakes of foxtail" is a variation of Richard Haydock's "The lockes or plaine feakes of haire called cow-lickes," from his translation of Gian Paolo Lomazzo's *A Tracte Containing the Artes of Curious Paintinge, Carvinge & Buildinge* (1598). Richard Haydock (ca. 1569–1642) was a physician and engraver who apparently coined the word "cowlick."

"Grass Veneer [1]": In taxonomy, *sensu lato* means "in the broadest sense." *Ad libitum* is a type of field-note sampling that is informal and without any systematic constraints.

"Forecast Issued 6:00 am CST...": "one for sorrow, two for mirth" is from a traditional English nursery rhyme about magpies.

The title "Occasionally the Field of Possibilities" is a phrase from Grinnell's "The Principle of Rapid Peering, in Birds."

"The Walk, or The Principle of Rapid Peering . . .": This poem makes several references to Robert Walser's *The Walk*, translated by Christopher Middleton with Susan Bernofsky, including "A Living Poem" (in the subtitle of my poem), which is a variation of his passage "A pleasant walk . . . teems with imageries, living poems." Other quotations from Walser include, in Part 1, "simplicity most ancient to walk on foot," and in Part 2, "the green and luscious embellishments of trees." The lines: "the first, short warble of spring is nearly thus" and "loose membership in the roving aggregation of birds" are from Thompson's *The Birds of Manitoba*. "The field of our work is the region immediately about us" is from Grinnell's "The Principle of Rapid Peering, in Birds," and the "rich acoustic world of moths / fallen silent" is a variation of a passage in David C. Lees and Alberto Zilli's *Moths: A Complete Guide to Biology and Behavior*. The phrase "the only moving thing" is from the second line of Wallace Stevens's "Thirteen Ways of Looking at a Blackbird."

"'False Chronologies with Birds and Moths'": The phrase "The dream inward . . ." is an allusion to Inger Christensen's essay "The Regulating Effect of Chance" in *The Condition of Secrecy*.

"Recollections of the Future": The title of this poem is from Miroslav Holub's essay "Sukhumi; or, Recollections of the Future" in *Shedding Life*.

*

The following works—many referenced in the notes above—were essential to my thinking about and researching this collection:

David Beadle and Seabrooke Leckie, *Peterson Field Guide to Moths of Northeastern North America* (Boston: Houghton Mifflin Harcourt, 2012).

David M. Bird, consultant editor, *Birds of Western Canada*, 2nd Edition (Toronto: DK/Penguin Random House, 2019).

Donna Bruce and Joan Feather, *A Guide to Nature Viewing Sites In and Around Saskatoon*, 3rd Edition (Saskatoon: Saskatoon Nature Society, 2016).

Inger Christensen, *The Condition of Secrecy*, translated by Susanna Nied (New York: New Directions, 2018).

Joseph Grinnell, *Philosophy of Nature, Selected Writings of a Western Naturalist* (Berkeley and Los Angeles: University of California Press, 1943).

Vernon Harms, Anna Leighton, and Mary Vetter, *Rushes, Bulrushes & Pondweeds plus the remaining Monocots of Saskatchewan* (Regina: Nature Saskatchewan, 2018).

Miroslav Holub, *Poems Before & After*, translated by Ian and Jarmila Milner, George Theiner, and Ewald Osers (Northumberland: Bloodaxe Books, 2006).

———, *Shedding Life: Disease, Politics, and Other Human Conditions*, translated by David Young (Minneapolis: Milkweed Editions, 1997).

David C. Lees and Alberto Zilli, *Moths: A Complete Guide to Biology and Behavior* (Washington, DC: Smithsonian Books, 2019).

Anna L. Leighton, *Sedges (Carex) of Saskatchewan* (Regina: Nature Saskatchewan, 2012).

Anna L. Leighton and Vernon L. Harms, *Grasses of Saskatchewan* (Regina: Nature Saskatchewan, 2014).

Jerry A. Powell and Paul A. Opler, *Moths of Western North America* (Berkeley and Los Angeles: University of California Press, 2009).

Alan Smith, *Saskatchewan Birds* (Edmonton: Lone Pine Publishing, 2020).

Ernest E. Thompson, *The Birds of Manitoba* (Washington, DC: Smithsonian Institution, 1891).

Robert Walser, *The Walk*, translated by Christopher Middleton with Susan Bernofsky (New York: New Directions, 2012).

Acknowledgments

"A Rolling Moth Etymology" first appeared in *The Yale Review* (Fall 2023).

Excerpts from "The Walk, or The Principle of Rapid Peering" first appeared in *Conjunctions Online* (July 2022) and *New American Writing* 41 (Summer 2023).

"Occasionally the Field of Possibilities" numbers 2, 4, 5, and 6 first appeared in *Chicago Review* 66:02 (Fall 2022).

"As If These Objects Were Moving and the Bird Itself Were Quiet," "These Birds and All Kindred Species That Roost in the Reeds," and "Take the Case of the Meadowlark" first appeared in *The Paris Review* 240 (Summer 2022).

"Forecast Issued 5:00 am CST . . ." and "Forecast Issued 6:00 am CST . . ." first appeared in *Harvard Review* 59 (Summer 2022).

"Voucher Specimen [1]" and "Voucher Specimen [2]" first appeared in *New American Writing* 40 (Summer 2022).

"A Melodic Expectation" and "Smell Giveaway (Threes on long stalks)" first appeared online at *This Singing Land* (thissingingland.ca) in the summer of 2021.

"Grass Veneer [1]" and "Grass Veneer [2]" first appeared in *Prairie Fire* (Spring 2021).

"Viscum Album" first appeared in *Conjunctions* 75 (Fall 2020).

*

I am grateful to the Canada Council for the Arts and to SK Arts for grants that helped with the completion of this collection.

Thank you to Susan Andrews Grace who told me I wasn't deluded thinking the poems were any good, and to Rachael Allen for her unwavering support of my work.

Many big (huge!) thank yous to everyone at New Directions, especially Jeffrey Yang, Barbara Epler, Declan Spring, Erik Rieselbach, Maya Solovej, and Mieke Chew. Thanks as well to Erik Carter for another brilliant cover (with eyespots!), and to Marian Bantjes for the beautiful interior design.

Sylvia Legris was born in Winnipeg, Manitoba. Her collection *Garden Physic* was chosen as one of the Best Poetry Books of the Year by *The* (London) *Times* and CBC/Radio-Canada. Her other poetry collections include *The Hideous Hidden*, *Pneumatic Antiphonal*, and *Nerve Squall*, winner of the Griffin Poetry Prize and the Pat Lowther Award. She lives in Saskatoon, Saskatchewan.